WISE & WACKY WACKY PROVERBS

THE TRUTH BEHIND EVERYDAY SAYINGS

JIM ANTON

Illustrated by Jean Anton

STERLING PUBLISHING CO., INC   NEW YORK

10 9 8 7 6 5 4 3 2 1

Published in 1996 by Sterling Publishing Company, Inc.
387 Park Avenue South, New York, N.Y. 10016
Originally published by Sterling Publishing in
hardcover as *The Sense and Nonsense of Proverbs*
© 1993 by Jim Anton & Jean Anton
Distributed in Canada by Sterling Publishing
% Canadian Manda Group, One Atlantic Avenue, Suite 105
Toronto, Ontario, Canada M6K 3E7
Distributed in Great Britain and Europe by Cassell PLC
Wellington House, 125 Strand, London WC2R 0BB, England
Distributed in Australia by Capricorn Link (Australia) Pty Ltd.
P.O. Box 6651, Baulkham Hills, Business Centre, NSW 2153, Australia
Manufactured in the United States of America

Sterling ISBN 0-8069-8485-6

Contents

Acknowledgments

We would like to thank the following people without whom this book would not have been possible: Kim Lemoi and Sara Jane Gabig, whose patient and objective criticism is much appreciated; Sheila Anne Barry, the editor who first accepted our proposal and presented it to Sterling; and Laurel Ornitz and Hannah Steinmetz, the editors who worked on the project and whose input was invaluable.

Introduction

Proverbs, sayings, and common expressions often have very long lives. For instance, the proverb "Art is long, life is short" originated about two thousand five hundred years ago in Greece. Since that time, the proverb has appeared throughout the centuries.

Proverbs often shed a special light on a human activity. In the above example, the proverb suggests that art deserves its elevated place in the human scheme of things because it often outlasts its creator. This wonderful insight into art was immediately accepted and continues to be appreciated to this day. Proverbs, like art, also outlive their creators.

Webster's Dictionary defines a proverb as a saying that is true. Common sense is often at the root of the proverb. It is common sense to say that "art is long and life is short." Perhaps this is another reason for the longevity and popularity of so many proverbs.

However, a scientific look at some proverbs, sayings, and expressions can show them from a very different angle. A scientific approach often gives new insights and helps to make other discoveries. For instance, it is possible that a biologist looking at the proverb "Art is long, life is short" might declare that life originated on earth more than three and a half billion years ago. What work of art is as old as that? Therefore, from the biologist's point of view, life is longer than art.

Looking at proverbs from other perspectives sheds new, stimulating light on them without detracting from their fundamental truths. This is one of the purposes of this book. Another purpose is simply to have fun.

COMPARISONS

As Constant As the North Star

In Shakespeare's play *Julius Caesar*, Caesar says:

> But I am constant as the northern star
> Of whose true-fix'd and resting quality
> There is no fellow in the firmament.

Caesar was probably referring to the fact that, unlike other stars that seem to move across the sky as the seasons change, the North Star doesn't seem to move at all. This is because it lies over the North Pole.

However, the earth wobbles on its axis. Because of this wobble, the North Star is not in the same place today that it was in when Caesar saw it.

The North Star also pulsates, because gases trapped inside it expand when they are heated up. As they expand, the star shines more brightly. After releasing some heat, it cools off, contracts, and shines less brightly.

The North Star has been pulsating for about 40,000 years. However, astronomers predict that will soon stop. Why? Simply because after it has lost a certain amount of heat, it won't be able to generate enough heat to cause it to expand.

So—the North Star moves and changes, invalidating the claim of its famous admirer, Julius Caesar.

A Fish Out of Water

If an Eskimo suddenly found himself in the tropics, he probably would feel out of place. Until he adjusted to the change, he might not feel "at home." He might feel like "a fish out of water."

A person who is "a fish out of water" is a misplaced person. But what about actual fish "out of water?" Are they always misplaced? As it turns out, some fish spend most of their lives out of water.

The salamanderfish is one example. This fish lives in western Australia. But don't look for it in any ponds. You would have a much better chance finding it buried in sand.

How does it live? It hollows out a hole for itself in the sand, and calls that hole home. Other fish in this situation would have trouble breathing. They use gills for breathing, and gills don't work out of water. But the salamander fish is different. It breathes through its skin.

How long can this fish live out of water? It can survive in the baking sand for up to four years! During this period of time, it does not eat, breed, or even swim!

What kind of life is that for a fish? Not a bad one when you consider the alternative. If the fish did not bury itself in the sand, it would die.

Every so often, the parched sand is flooded with rain. When this happens, little ponds form. The ponds may last from weeks to months. Within hours the two-inch salamanderfish emerges from its sandy home. It swims, eats, breeds, and, yes, even breathes like other fish, by using its gills.

When the pond dries up, what happens?

The salamanderfish goes back to being a fish out of water.

Blind As a Bat

Are bats really blind?

Bats are creatures of the night. They hunt for insects and pollinate flowers under a cloak of darkness. Bats and all other nocturnal creatures know that nighttime is the best time to avoid being seen by predators.

But how do bats get around in the dark? They use echolocation, bouncing sound off an object and then creating an actual image of the object from the sound. In other words, bats can see with their ears!

However, "ear sight" is not the only kind of sight that bats possess. Most bats also have excellent eyesight.

So bats are *not* blind twice over. They can see not only with their ears but also with their eyes.

Cave fish, which live in darkness, are totally blind. Komodo dragons are nearly blind. So, blind as a cave fish or a komodo dragon would be a more accurate phrase.

Bird Brain

Birds are not respected for their intelligence. Maybe that is why it is not very flattering to be called a "bird brain."

But are birds as stupid as they are reputed to be?

Some birds, such as domestic turkeys, admittedly do not have a lot of smarts. On the other hand, crows are a different story. Their survival depends on brains.

Crows hide their food. They do this because other birds simply have no respect for personal property. But as much as six months to a year later, when crows need food, they can find their hidden stash.

How do they do it? It can't be their sense of smell. If they could smell the hidden food, so could any other crow or many other birds. They actually cover their hiding place with leaves, sand, and twigs so that the fragrance of their food is eliminated or at least camouflaged.

They are able to find their food by remembering where they hid it! Have you ever put something away, and then forgotten where you put it? That doesn't happen to crows. They can remember exactly where they hid their food six months to a year later!

Crows are not the only birds which have good memories—so do jays, chickadees, and woodpeckers, among others. So, when you call someone a "bird brain," you may or may not be accurate. It depends on what bird you're talking about.

As the Crow Flies

"As the crow flies" is another way of saying that the shortest distance between two points is a straight line.

But is it really?

If you have to fly from Los Angeles to New York, what would be the shortest route? At first you might think, a straight line. However, the earth is not flat. An airplane actually follows the curvature of the earth, so it flies along a curve, not a straight line.

The shortest distance *would be* a straight line if the airplane could fly *through* the earth to New York instead of over it, right?

Not according to Albert Einstein.

According to his theory, the shortest distance between two places is *always* a curve, not a straight line. Space, he said, is curved. Even if the earth were filled with space, to get from one place to another you would have to follow a curve.

Hence, when you say to get somewhere "as the crow flies," you're really not talking about a straight line.

Eats Like a Bird

If a person is a poor eater, we say the person "eats like a bird." But are birds really poor eaters?

Most birds eat all day long. Many of them eat the equivalent of their own weight in food every day!

Birds eat so much because they fly. Flying seems like fun from the human point of view; however, flight requires energy. Lots of it. In order to fly, birds spend the majority of their time fueling up.

Therefore, when we say, "So-and-so eats like a bird," we are giving a left-handed compliment. To eat like a bird, a person might have to eat a hundred or more pounds of food a day!

Crocodile Tears

One of the earliest references to "crocodile tears" occurs in Shakespeare's *Othello*. In that famous play, Othello says of the unfortunate Desdemona, "Each drop she falls would prove a crocodile." In other words, Othello believes that his wife's tears are not real, and that they are shed to deceive him into thinking that she feels an emotion that does not really exist. He believes that her tears are as false as those of a crocodile.

But do crocodiles shed "false tears" or any tears at all, for that matter? Production of tears depends on the crocodile. Freshwater crocodiles produce no tears at all. Saltwater crocodiles, on the other hand, need to produce tears for their survival.

The tears shed by saltwater crocodiles are similar to the tears shed by birds, such as the albatross, that spend long periods of time over the sea. They have no source of fresh water and so must resort to drinking seawater. Drinking seawater, however, could be fatal if it were not for the special tear glands that these animals possess. These glands filter out the salt from the water and then excrete the salt in concentrated droplets, or tears.

Thus, actual crocodile tears are no more attached to emotions than the fake tears that people sometimes produce—though they do have a much more respectable purpose.

Cold Fish

Fish are cold-blooded animals. A person who shows little or no emotion, no matter what the situation, is sometimes called a "cold fish."

However, cold is a relative term when it comes to fish. Unlike mammals and birds, which are able to maintain a nearly constant body temperature, a fish's body temperature is nearly the same as the water in which it lives. Since some fish live in very cold environments and other fish live in relatively warm ones, their average body temperatures may vary quite widely. However, cold fish probably perceive the world to be no colder than do warmer fish. Each is equally active and happy to be alive at its respective water temperature.

Drinks Like a Fish

We say that a person "drinks like a fish" when he or she drinks too much.

But do fish actually drink a lot?

Fish do take a great deal of water into their mouths, but almost all of it passes right through them and out their gills. Very little water is swallowed. They don't need to drink a lot of water because fish don't sweat. Their purpose in taking in water is to obtain oxygen for breathing. Fish need oxygen to produce energy.

Fish actually drink less than many other vertebrates.

Hungry As a Bear

Bears spend a great deal of time hibernating. During this period, their heart rate, respiration rate, and metabolism slow down much more than they do when they are only sleeping.

Hibernation lasts for the harsh months of winter. It is the bear's way of coping with barren living conditions. "Wake me up when there's something around to eat" is the strategy behind this behavior.

During hibernation, bears do not get up even to urinate or defecate. Since they have not eaten anything all winter, they lose a lot of weight. They have been living off the fat of their body for the entire period.

When spring comes, bears not only have to consume enough food to lead a normal, active life, but they also must prepare for the time when they will have to hibernate. This necessity makes them very hungry animals, indeed.

Hence, if you say you're as "hungry as a bear," you're talking about a voracious appetite.

Eyes Like an Eagle

Do eagles really have the best eyesight?

It hasn't been proven, since no one has tested the eyesight of all animals. However, eagles would surely be at the top of the list. It is known, for example, that the golden eagle, *Aquila chrysaetos*, can spot a rabbit from two miles away!

Having eyes like an eagle does have a disadvantage. In order to have such good vision, the eyeball of the eagle is elongated. This means that the eyeball cannot move around in its socket.

If we had eyes like eagles, we could see a rabbit from far away, but in order to see something off to one side, we'd have to turn our entire head instead of just our eyes.

Free As a Bird

Who hasn't wished to be as "free as a bird"?

But our fine-feathered friends are not as carefree as they may seem. In fact, most birds are pretty anxious creatures. For one thing, they have to be on constant lookout for cats, birds of prey, and human enemies. For another, most birds spend a lot of time feeding and caring for their young. For instance, a pair of birds called great tits, *Parus major*, were observed feeding their chicks more than 1,200 times *in a single day*. This came after many days of collecting materials for a nest, and spending still more time and energy building it.

Migrating, sometimes thousands of miles, is necessary for the survival of some bird species. Birds on such prolonged flights run a pretty good risk of losing their lives. They don't really choose to migrate; they migrate because they have to.

At the end of a hard day at work, if you have to shop for groceries on the way home, then cook dinner, and put your children to bed, you're still probably much freer than most birds.

Like a Chicken Without Its Head

We say that a person is running around like "a chicken without its head" when he or she appears to be acting without thinking and seems confused.

As a matter of fact, a decapitated chicken may actually run around for a few seconds without its head before finally kicking the bucket. This is because chicken reflexes continue to operate for some time after decapitation. Reflexes do not need a brain to operate. Sensory neurons, the spinal cord, and motor neurons take charge without the supervision of a brain.

Of course, the decapitated animal knows not where it is running and is indeed confused. Hence, the saying is literally, if not morbidly, true.

Laughs Like a Hyena

The spotted hyena is best known for its "laughter." However, hyena "laughing" is no laughing matter. The hyena makes a laughing sound when it is being chased or attacked. That eerie sound of hysterical laughter is actually a cry.

So, if you say that someone "laughs like a hyena," you'd only be accurate if he or she sounded hysterical and was frightened.

HA HA HA
HEE HEE

Lone Wolf

The "lone wolf" is the person who "goes it alone." We generally admire "lone wolves" for their independence. John Wayne riding off into the sunset may be a modern archetype for the "lone wolf."

However, from the wolf's point of view, the saying has different connotations.

Wolves grow up in a family. They remain with their family until it is time for them to start a family of their own. This is because wolves are social animals and they have a better chance of survival in a pack than individually.

The "lone wolf" may be a human, or at least an American, hero. But from the standpoint of the wolf, a lone wolf is an unhappy, more vulnerable creature.

If John Wayne had been an actual wolf, the other wolves might have felt sorry for him.

Mad As a Hatter

Ever since the Middle Ages, people have noticed that the incidence of insanity among hatters is much higher than it is in the general public.

This is because hat makers use mercury in the manufacture of felt hats and mercury is extremely toxic. It adversely affects both the brain and the nervous system. Hatters who work with mercury inhale its vapor and absorb small quantities through their skin. The mercury then travels to the brain. As a result, it is not uncommon for hatters who work with mercury to go mad.

Therefore, when we say that someone is as "mad as a hatter," we're referring to a phenomenon that has supposedly gone on for hundreds of years.

Hatters are not the only group of professionals affected by mercury. Chemists and other scientists are also affected sometimes. This is perhaps the origin of the other saying, "mad scientist."

Slow As a Turtle

Not all turtles are as slow as you may think.

For instance, in 1939 a leatherback turtle was clocked at 22.4 miles per hour. It must have really been in a hurry. Normal cruising speed for this animal is about four miles per hour. However, the above-mentioned leatherback, which lives in the sea, was swimming, not walking.

Tests on land-dwelling tortoises show that even when hungry and enticed by food, the tortoise, *Geochelone gigantea*, could not move more than .17 miles per hour.

However, neither turtles nor tortoises are the slowest land mammals. The slowest recorded land mammal is the three-toed sloth, *Bradypus tridactylus*. On the ground it zips along at a top speed of .09 miles per hour.

Mad As a March Hare

In *Alice in Wonderland* by Lewis Carroll, Alice wonders if she should visit the March Hare or the Mad Hatter. She decides to visit the March Hare, and she gives the following reason: ". . . perhaps, as this is May, the March Hare won't be raving mad—at least not so mad as it was in March."

But are hares really mad in March?

This question was investigated by zoologists Anthony Holley and Paul Greenwood at the University of Durham, in England. They discovered that the mad-hare behavior referred to by Alice actually consists of hares chasing each other and boxing. But to their surprise, they found that males never boxed with other males. Instead, the boxing matches occurred between males and females.

Why do hares of opposite sexes box?

Females box, they found, to prevent certain males from mating with them.

However, Alice was wrong about March.

Hares (known for their prodigious mating behavior) are nearly always at it. Besides March, they also go "mad" in January, February, April, May, June, July, and August.

So, the March hare is just as mad in May as it is in March.

Wise As an Owl

Owls have some special gifts, but are they wise?

They can turn their heads around 180 degrees. They also have excellent eyesight especially suited to night vision, and they can fly in nearly absolute silence. These adaptations make them formidable predators.

However, there is no evidence that they are more intelligent than other birds.

Memory Like an Elephant

The origin of this saying is unknown.

Maybe it came about because of the size of the elephant's brain. For instance, an Asiatic elephant's brain weighs as much as 16.5 pounds (7.5 kilograms). This much mass makes the brain of an elephant the biggest brain of all land animals.

Another possibility is that the saying may refer to the myth of elephant burial grounds. Elephants allegedly remember where their burial grounds are, and go there to die.

However, after years of investigation, researchers have been unable to verify this behavior in elephants. So-called elephant burial grounds may be no more than places where several elephants had perished together by chance.

Chimps have better memories than elephants. It would be far better to have a memory like a chimp than like an elephant.

Sings Like a Bird

Most birds don't sing.

Singing, among our feathered friends, is confined primarily to the males, which eliminates about fifty percent of all birds. The males sing for a variety of reasons. Some are singing songs of "love"; they are trying to obtain a mate. Others are singing words of warning: "You are in my territory," for example. "Keep away!"

Birds are not the only animals that sing. So do frogs, whales, crickets, and newts. Newt songs sound a little like the squeak produced when a wet finger is run along glass. But as far as female newts are concerned, music is what the newt is making. For that matter, wolves also sing. We just don't call what they do singing. We call it howling.

And then there are those birds that do not sing very well at all. For instance, parrots and parakeets may be known for their ability to mimic human sound, but they have terrible-sounding singing voices. Woodpeckers don't sing at all. They communicate by tapping on wood. The tapping seems to attract female woodpeckers the same way that singing attracts female canaries.

When we say that someone "sings like a bird," we mean that he or she has a pleasing voice—and there is nothing technically wrong with the saying, as long as it refers to certain male birds.

To Change Like a Chameleon

A "chameleon" is a person who alters his or her outward attitudes and behavior to suit circumstances. For instance, the person would act one way with one person and completely differently with another.

The saying "to change like a chameleon" is based on the belief that chameleons can change colors to match their particular environment.

But can they?

Chameleons do change color. But the change is a response to fear, anger, or some other excitement. Often the change causes the animal to blend in with its environment. This adaptation in response to fear is an important survival mechanism. However, alter the chameleon's environment and the changing-color routine may not work.

For instance, if a chameleon is placed in a blue box, it will change to brown when excited. It changed color all right, but not to any advantage. In the blue environment, the change would make it more visible, not less.

The chameleon simply cannot match *any* setting. It might take thousands of years of natural selection for it to match a new environment.

Scaredy Cat

A "scaredy cat" is someone who is "afraid of his or her own shadow." In other words, a "scaredy cat" is a kind of coward.

But are cats particularly cowardly?

Sometimes house cats seem to get "spooked" rather easily. However, zoologists explain this behavior as a response to overwhelming stimuli rather than as a lack of courage. Cats are very attuned to their immediate environment and, normally, take time to sort out all the stimuli before they act. When surprises overwhelm their senses, they appear to be frightened.

But they are not necessarily scared; sometimes the most prudent response is to make yourself scarce in a hurry.

Sweats Like a Pig

When it is hot, we sweat. But are we, in fact, "sweating like pigs"?

As it turns out, pigs are falsely maligned by this common saying. Pigs may do some awful things, but they don't sweat. They can't. Pigs don't have sweat glands.

Living without sweat glands isn't easy. Sweating is nature's evaporative cooler. As sweat evaporates from the skin, it carries unwanted heat with it.

So, how do pigs cool themselves? They wallow. By rolling in mud, they cover their skin with a nice, cool coat of muddy insulation. This mud coat keeps the sun from burning their nearly naked skin. Also, since the mud is wet to begin with, the water in it evaporates, and, as it does so, it carries off unwanted heat.

The next time you hear someone say, "He sweats like a pig," you might suggest that "sweats like a cow or a horse" would be much more accurate. Cows and horses sweat as profusely as pigs are erroneously purported to do.

White Elephant

"White elephant" is a term that is often used to describe a house or other possession that can't be sold because it is too expensive to maintain.

The term comes from a myth about a king of Siam who allegedly presented a white elephant to a courtier whom he disliked. White elephants were regarded as sacred by certain religious groups in Siam. However, the king gave the white elephant to his enemy for a malevolent purpose. Feeding and caring for the elephant would take up so much of the courtier's time that he would be ruined financially. And since the white elephant was sacred, he could not get rid of it easily.

Actual white elephants, or albinos, are unable to produce enough pigment to block the sun's ultraviolet radiation. White elephants, therefore, need even more care than normal elephants. Since elephants generally spend a great deal of time in the open sun, white elephants find survival much more of a challenge. For this reason, they are uncommon in the wild.

Actual white elephants, while different and therefore special, are as burdensome to themselves as "white-elephant" homes are to their owners.

BEST
WISHES,
THE KING

Sneaky As a Weasel

It is not a compliment to call someone a "weasel." A "weasel" generally refers to a person who is sneaky, untrustworthy, and dishonest.

But are we being fair to weasels?

Weasels are members of the mustelid group. Mustelid means mouse catcher. Weasels, which are the smallest carnivores, eat mice. If it weren't for weasels, many places would be overrun by mice.

Weasels also attack animals up to six times their own size. This would be like a 200-pound man without a weapon attacking a 1,200-pound animal.

Weasel fur, which turns white in winter, is called ermine. At one time, only kings and queens and members of the royal family were permitted to wear ermine.

When we say someone is a weasel, we are comparing a sneaky, untrustworthy person to a strong, very brave, and quite beautiful animal.

How, then, did weasels get such a negative reputation? Perhaps it's because if you were a farmer, you would not trust the brave little critter in your chicken coop.

ADVICE

All That Glitters Is Not Gold

Anyone who has ever seen pyrite, or fool's gold, knows what it looks like. It looks like gold. But it is not the real thing.

But if something looks like gold, what difference does it make whether or not it is really gold?

Gold has a special property that sets it apart from almost all other metals. Gold is one of the few metals that does not combine with oxygen. Iron is at the other end of the metallic spectrum. It readily combines with oxygen. That's why iron turns into rust. Copper turns green when it combines with oxygen. Silver turns black. But nothing happens to gold.

Gold is valued not only for its initial glitter, but also because no matter how old it is, it *continues* to glitter. Hence, if it is a yellow metal and it glitters, but does not keep on glittering, it is not gold.

This proverb is a warning: Take a long look; appearances may be deceiving!

A Bird in the Hand Is Worth Two in the Bush

What birds in which bushes?

In the Middle Ages, trappers went out and beat actual bushes with sticks or branches cut from trees. The purpose was to drive out any birds that were in the bushes. If the trappers got lucky, the birds were caught with a net, and sold at the market the next day.

What are the birds doing in bushes?

They live there. Most birds are diurnal creatures; they hunt for food, search for mates, and build nests during the day. At night, bush-dwelling birds are doing what other diurnal creatures are doing. They are catching seven winks.

The proverb originated in fifteenth-century England. It is better to accept what you have than to try to get more and risk losing everything is the gist of the saying.

All Work and No Play Makes Jack a Dull Boy

Is play really as important as this seventeenth-century English proverb makes it out to be? According to zoologists, it is, and not just for people but also for animals.

When a dog chases a stick, it is play-hunting. The stick represents its catch. When the dog brings the stick back to its master, it is pretending to be sharing its catch with its pack. Chimpanzees sometimes bang on a can just to make noise. They too are playing.

Another form of animal play is the play-fight. Young monkeys and bear cubs wrestle. Puppies tumble with each other and play-bite. Kittens tease and run.

Why do young animals play? One reason is that it increases bonding among them. It gives them an opportunity to form groups. Later, when they get older, these groups become an essential part of their life. Play also allows animals to practise skills that they may need later, as adults.

All work and no play would make Cheetah, Fido, or Felix as dull as Jack.

Dead Men Tell No Tales

This proverb dates back to 1664: " 'Twere best To knock 'um i' th' head. . . . The dead can tell no tales," in *Andronicus Comnenius* by John Wilson.

The eerie truth behind this proverb, that a dead person is not about to tell anything to anyone, was undebatable, at least until the twentieth century.

Then DNA technology came along.

A victim is murdered and no witnesses are present. Perhaps a dead person could tell no tales in the seventeenth century; however, sometimes all it takes in the twentieth century to uncover a murderer is a single cell. DNA fingerprinting from a single cell could establish conclusively that the murderer was at the scene of the crime.

Apart from murder, twentieth-century molecular biologists can determine what a dead man ate, what drugs he took, as well as who his ancestors were from a follicle of hair.

He Laughs Best Who Laughs Last

This proverb, from the early seventeenth century, implies that it is always important to think about the long-range victory; the short-term victory may not turn out to be too good in the end.

But why laugh at all?

Physiologists have actually discovered that laughter is good for our health. It reduces stress, which helps the immune system.

Laughter also produces endorphins, certain chemicals in the brain that help reduce pain and give a person a feeling of well-being. When we laugh, nearly every organ in our body is exercised. Blood vessels relax, which helps reduce blood pressure.

Some hospitals have incorporated humor in the form of videotapes or TV shows into the schedules of recovering patients. Some have gone so far as to hire comedians to cause patients to laugh. The hospitals report that laughing often helps sick people to recover more quickly.

A word has even been created for the science of laughter: gelotology.

As far as physiologists can tell, he (or she) who laughs *most* may live longest.

Constant Dropping Wears Away a Stone

This proverb dates back to the fifth century B.C., where it is found in a manuscript of the Greek writer Choerilus.

It is a metaphor for persistence. Just as water can wear away stone, so too can patient, constant effort achieve a difficult or unlikely end.

In nature, the Grand Canyon is a good example of the literal truth of this proverb. Two factors led to the existence of the Grand Canyon, which is one mile deep, 277 miles long, and as wide as 18 miles. The first is the land at the bottom of the canyon, which is slowly rising. The second is the Colorado River, which has constantly flowed there. As time passes, the Colorado River cuts through the rising earth like a knife cutting through cheese.

The Grand Canyon is the result of a constant wearing away of earth and stone.

The Apple Never Falls Far from the Tree

Since a falling apple is propelled by gravity, it falls straight down. Therefore, you would think you could tell what kind of tree the seeds of this apple would produce by examining the tree it is under.

However, if such an apple remained under the "mother," it probably would produce no tree at all.

In order to develop into a tree, the seeds need to be planted far from the "mother" tree. Otherwise, the emerging sapling would be forced to compete with it for sunlight and water. Considering the size of the bigger tree's branches and root system, the smaller tree would not have much of a chance.

In order to be successful, the apple would have to roll far enough away (which may account for why apples are round) or be carried off by an animal and deposited somewhere, where it would not have to compete for survival.

But the proverb is not really about apples. It is about people. It suggests that one can predict how a child will turn out by looking at the parents. Chances are, says the proverb, the child will be like them.

However, every child is different from its parents. This is because we each possess combinations of genes unique to us. This genetic combination has never existed before in the history of life and most likely will never exist again.

Don't Count Your Chickens Before They Hatch

The advice this proverb is offering is that you should not make or act upon an assumption (generally favorable) that might turn out to be wrong—*you never know.* Chickens produce far more eggs than are expected to survive.

Chickens are not alone here.

In the wild, overproduction is a species' way of guaranteeing its survival, no matter how the environment changes.

For instance, the ocean sunfish produces 300 million eggs. In a stable habitat, only two eggs would survive to adulthood—just enough to replace the parents. The same is true of the conger eel, which produces 15 million eggs, and the carp, which produces as many as two million.

Counting any kind of offspring before they hatch is almost always disappointing.

An Apple a Day Keeps the Doctor Away

This English proverb dates from the nineteenth century. The original version is "Eat an apple on going to bed, and you'll keep the doctor from earning his bread."

Apples contain vitamins A and C as well as the minerals iron, phosphorus, and calcium. But do apples really do anything for your health?

If you had no other source of vitamin C, apples certainly would help keep the doctor away. We need vitamin C to clot blood and for other vital functions. However, lemons and limes are much richer in vitamin C than apples are.

As far as keeping the doctor away, garlic and onions would be much more effective than apples. They contain sulfur compounds that actually destroy bacterial and fungal infections. Apples, on the other hand, have virtually no effect against these infections.

So, if you need vitamin C and cannot get citrus fruits, then maybe an apple a day would keep the doctor away.

But, in most other cases, you'd be better off eating a clove of raw garlic every day. The problem is, not only would it keep the doctor away, but probably everyone else as well.

Even an Ass Won't Fall in the Same Quicksand Twice

Don't make the same mistake twice is the meaning of this proverb.

However, quicksand is not all that it has been made out to be. The deadly quicksand concept was dreamed up in the movies. How many times have you seen across the screen quicksand suck a person below its surface? But in reality it cannot. If a heavy object were placed on top of quicksand, it would sink as it would in water, only a little more slowly.

If you can swim, swimming out of quicksand is about as easy as swimming out of water. Even if you can't swim, then floating could save you. It is easier to float on quicksand than it is on water.

So, it may be true that even an ass wouldn't fall in the same quicksand twice. But not to worry anyway, it's easy enough to get out of quicksand—unless you're in the movies.

Two Heads Are Better Than One

One person has an idea; a second person could likely contribute something new or useful to it. That is the gist of this fourteenth-century proverb.

But, in nature, are two heads better than one?

Not at least when it comes to the planaria, a flatworm. This animal has amazing powers of regeneration. For instance, by splitting its head lengthwise, each side can grow a new half. In a relatively short time, the formally normal worm is turned into a two-headed monster.

Is it any better off?

Apparently not. Planarian heads will sometimes disagree on which direction to go. In such cases, it literally heads off in different directions, actually tearing its body in two. Each half then grows back the missing parts.

A two-headed snake lives at the department of zoology of Arizona State University. It has four eyes, two mouths, two brains, and so on. Luckily it lives in a tank. In the wild, this snake probably would not last as long as a normal, single-headed member of its species.

In a literal sense, two heads are not better than one, otherwise more animals would have them.

Might Makes Right

But why doesn't might make left?

Less than one hundred years ago, it wasn't considered right to be left-anything. For instance, it was believed to be unnatural to be left-handed, and left-handed people even were forced to learn to be right-handed.

About ninety percent of all people are right-handed and about ten percent are left-handed, with less than one percent being truly ambidextrous.

But how does this explain why we say something is right rather than left? Ninety percent of us are righties, so righties have "won" by sheer force of numbers.

In other words, might really did make right *right*. But is justice really nothing more than the interests of the stronger?

Don't Make Waves

We "make waves" by disturbing the status quo. If you have a choice in a situation, the saying goes, "Don't make waves."

However, oceanographers have a different point of view about waves entirely. In order to study them, they may spend years in a laboratory with a ripple tank making waves.

Nature also makes waves. Waves begin their existence in the open sea as little ripples. These ripples are formed by gentle sea breezes. In the open sea, if the wind continues blowing, the ripples grow into waves. Continued wind causes little waves to catch up to other little waves. The combined force causes them to grow into one big wave.

Waves can also be caused by tides or underwater earthquakes. Such great waves, called tsunamis, may travel ten thousand miles before reaching their full height and destiny.

Both in nature and in real-life situations, making waves is sometimes not a matter of choice.

There's Safety in Numbers

This proverb can be supported by observing schools of fish, flocks of birds, or herds of animals. In each of these examples, more advantages are to be gained by being in a group than by "going it alone."

Fish that school as well as birds that form flocks are almost always preyed on by other animals. They live in groups because a group of a hundred animals has two hundred eyes looking out for predators. They also have a hundred noses ready to detect the faintest whiff of odor from a predator.

A group is also sometimes seen by predators as a single organism rather than as individuals. Sometimes a fierce predator will stay away from a group for this reason.

Why don't all animals form flocks or schools?

Simply because it is not always advantageous to be part of a group. For instance, a school, flock, or herd of predators would be at a severe disadvantage approaching prey. They would be easily seen before they could get into striking range.

So, while there may be safety in numbers, this policy depends on the type of animal and what it is doing—the same is probably true of people.

The Early Bird Catches the Worm

This proverb, which originated in the seventeenth century, seems reasonable enough. If a person gets somewhere first, that person obtains whatever there is to be obtained.

But is it true for birds?

Most birds go out as soon as possible after sunrise to find worms and other things to eat. But actually worms are more likely to emerge from their burrows at night.

Earthworms, for example, must stay underground all day because direct sunlight would dry up the moisture on their skin. Since they breathe through their moist skin, which absorbs oxygen, drying up would mean death.

The early bird, therefore, catches the occasional worm that for one reason or another is out in the morning when it should be underground.

APPEARANCES

Birds of a Feather Flock Together

This proverb, which first appeared in the Bible, Ecclesiasticus 13:16, means that you can judge a person by the company he or she keeps. If you want to know what type of person so-and-so is, take a close look at the person's friends. Chances are they have a lot in common.

What about actual birds "of a feather"? Do they flock together? Can they be judged by the company they keep?

Birds "of a feather" are the same type of bird; in other words, they are members of the same species. About 8,000 bird species are known. Only about 4,000 of these form flocks. The other 4,000 never flock at all.

However, sometimes birds that are *not* "of a feather" flock together. For example, species of herons and wrens will sometimes form a single flock.

So, it probably would be accurate to say that sometimes birds of a feather flock together, sometimes birds of a feather do not flock together, and finally, birds that are not of a feather sometimes flock together.

Therefore, you cannot always judge a bird by the company it keeps.

A Big Nose Never Spoilt a Handsome Face

A good case in point is the sperm whale, which many people would agree is a very handsome animal—despite its huge nose.

The sperm whale has the world's biggest nose. It can weigh as much as eight thousand pounds. The sperm whale's nose is full of a special oil that serves as a kind of flotation device. The oil, which is less dense than the rest of the animal, causes it to rise to the surface of the ocean after deep-diving for food.

The whale's nose also functions as a "hearing aid." It uses it to listen to songs and messages of other whales that may be thousands of miles away. Long-distance communication would be impossible without it.

Not only would the sperm whale find life difficult without its nose, but it probably would not be recognizable. Its nose takes up a full one-third of its body.

You might feel that a big nose is all well and good for a sperm whale, but what about for a person? Consider, then, Cyrano de Bergerac. He felt that his nose ruined his face. However, recall that the beautiful Roxanne did not find it cause for loving him less.

But this saying is not just about noses. Metaphorically, it means that something large and obtrusive on a beautiful person does not necessarily mean the ruination of what is already beautiful.

Seeing Things

People who wonder if they are "seeing things" are afraid that they are hallucinating, or seeing something that has no basis in reality.

A classic case occurs in a Bob Hope and Bing Crosby movie, *The Road to Morocco*. The two friends are stranded in the desert. Suddenly an oasis appears. Hope dives in, only to find that the oasis is not real. He emerges with a mouthful of sand, and wonders if the heat is affecting his mind.

The character was not hallucinating. He had seen a mirage. Mirages are real, and they are not uncommon in the desert.

Mirages are caused by refracting beams of light. Since the air just above the desert is hotter than air that is higher up in the atmosphere, the beams of light hitting it are bent. As a result, an upside-down image of the sky appears on the sand. This image looks like water. The shiny spot on a hot, dry highway that looks like water is also a mirage.

It used to be said that the way you could tell if something is a mirage is to try to take its picture. Mirages, it was said, could not be photographed. However, that saying is not true. Mirages appear even in photographs.

Which is further proof that if we see a mirage, we are not "seeing things."

A Chip off the Old Block

A chip from a block of cement or wood would be identical in composition to the original piece. The saying implies that the same is true about people. In fact, some of us seem a lot like one of our parents.

But it is impossible to have much more than fifty percent in common with one parent because we inherit about fifty percent of our genes from *each* parent.

Everybody has characteristics of both parents, but sometimes it is not so obvious.

We may seem to resemble a particular parent because of some obvious, dominant trait, such as black hair or brown eyes. However, a careful look at our genes would inevitably reveal that we possess traits that are foreign to both our parents. This apparent anomaly is possible because of recessive genes—genes that represent traits that are present but not operative in either parent. So, it would be possible to have blue eyes, even though both of our parents and their parents had brown eyes.

In any case, no one is a chip off the old block. It would be more accurate to say we are a conglomerate of a long line of ancestral blocks, each of which contributed something to the final product, which we refer to as us.

The Odd Man Out

"The odd man out" is the person who is quite different from the rest.

This saying is about as literally true as it can be when applied in a broad sense to the human animal. In his book *The Naked Ape*, Desmond Morris counts one hundred and ninety-three species of monkeys and apes on the planet (many of which are today endangered). One hundred and ninety-two of them are covered with hair.

The only naked primate is man.

Man is truly "the odd man out."

Beauty Fades Like a Flower

But why does beauty fade at all?

Like all the other characteristics of living things, beauty is an adaptation for survival. And like most adaptations, it is concerned not so much with the individual as with the species.

Flowers fade because they have served their purpose. Flowers are plants' reproductive organs. Once fertilized, they are no longer needed, so they are discarded, beautiful as they may be.

Beauty serves much the same purpose in higher living things. Though standards of beauty differ among animals, the underlying concept remains the same. Beauty could be defined as that which causes an animal to be sexually attractive. For a male elk, the size and number of points on his antlers determines his beauty. Swallows have long tail feathers, tropical fish have bright colors, and so on.

Since the offspring of higher animals require more care, older animals are less able to bear and rear them. Therefore, it is natural for a higher animal's beauty to fade as it grows older.

Fading beauty may at first seem like some kind of cruel joke. But if beauty serves no purpose, nature discards it. Waste not, want not.

Spitting Image

The term "spitting image" means that one individual is the mirror image of another. Identical twins seem to be the "spitting image" of each other. But how identical are they?

You might think they have to be identical in every way. After all, they were both formed from the same fertilized egg. However . . .

John and James Brick are physicians who practise medicine in West Virginia, and they are identical twins. If they are truly identical, you would think they would be more or less the same size. The trouble is, they aren't.

John has a much bigger waistline than James. He also has a bigger appetite. These differences have been true all their lives! If waistline and appetite are determined at birth, as most geneticists think, why should one identical twin have always been heavier than the other?

Geneticists are not exactly sure why some identical twins differ from their "identical" siblings. However, they are pretty sure that whatever it was that occurred, it happened *after* the egg split!

Waistline is not the only known difference between identical twins. There are cases where one identical twin is born with Down's syndrome and the other isn't. Down's syndrome means that the person has one too many chromosomes. Also, identical twins always have different fingerprints from one another.

So, despite popular sentiment, identical twins are actually never the "spitting image" of each other.

Red Alert

"Red alert" in the military signifies the most serious of situations. It is the last warning before action.

The choice of the color red by military leaders to signify danger is no accident. You don't have to be in the military to understand that the color red has special significance.

Red has a unique role in nature. It is a natural warning signal. Poison snakes, butterflies, frogs, and beetles display red to alert enemies.

For this reason, brightly colored animals often make no attempt to hide from potential predators. They carry their warning signals with them.

In nature, red means, "You've been warned."

You Are What You Eat

This modern proverb suggests that what we eat determines not only the general state of our health but also our attitude or manner. But how much of what we eat are we?

What we eat is reprocessed before becoming us. For instance, if we eat pork, we don't become pig-like. Instead, pork protein is broken down into amino acids. The amino acids are reassembled into human protein. The same holds true for chicken, beef, etc.

Nor do vegetarians necessarily become more gentle or plant-like. Hitler was a vegetarian; need one say more?

However, sometimes we may become what we eat. For instance, physicians think that eating foods high in cholesterol may lead to cholesterol buildup in our blood vessels, which leads to high blood pressure and heart disease.

In the animal kingdom, the monarch butterfly eats milkweed when it is a caterpillar. Milkweed contains cardenolide, a toxin that is extremely bitter to taste. The toxin becomes part of the butterfly even after the animal metamorphoses from a caterpillar.

The toxin protects it from predation by birds who've quickly learned that monarchs, being toxic and terrible-tasting, are what they eat.

What's in a Name?

Everything has a name. However, names can be deceiving.

For instance, the word jellyfish contains the word "fish." But jellyfish are not fish; they are cnidarians. Fish have scales and gills, to name only a few differences.

There are numerous other examples. The koala bear isn't a bear. It is cuddly and cute-looking, just as bears are, but it is a closer relative to a kangaroo than to a bear. Prairie dogs, on the other hand, are not dogs at all. They are closer to rats than to dogs. Horned toads, which have the nasty habit of squirting blood from their eyes at curious onlookers, aren't really toads. They aren't even amphibians. They are lizards. More obviously, sea lions are not lions, and sea cows aren't cows. Sea cows are much more closely related to elephants than to cows. Of course, sea monkeys aren't monkeys. They aren't even mammals; they are insects. Sea cucumbers aren't vegetables; they are relatives of starfish, which aren't fish. Both sea cucumbers and starfish are echinoderms. Not to mention seahorses. . . .

So, what's in a name? Not much.

The proverb is as true today as when it was written by Shakespeare in *Romeo and Juliet*.

SKY AND SPACE

Time Flies

But not for Einstein.

This proverb, first written by Chaucer in 1390 in *The Clerk's Tale*, expresses the surprise we all feel when we realize how quickly the years seem to go by. As we grow older, time seems to pass even more quickly than when we were young.

Why should this be?

When we are young, a year is a large percentage of our lives. For a ten-year-old child, one year is ten percent of a lifetime. However, for an eighty-year-old man, that same year is only about one percent of his lifetime.

But in his famous theory of relativity, Einstein proved that time can actually slow down. For instance, if we could travel near the speed of light, time would slow down and we would hardly age at all. This prediction was proved by atomic clocks on speedy jet aircraft. When the jets landed, less time had passed aboard them than did on earth.

At light speed (which is the fastest speed possible in the universe), time doesn't fly at all.

May the Force Be with You!

This saying first appeared in the film *Star Wars*. Its mythical implications are still with us. But is any literal, measurable "eternal" force actually still with us?

Scientists tell us there is.

The earth rotates on its axis once every day. The entire solar system is also rotating on its axis; so are the Milky Way galaxy and all the other galaxies in the entire universe!

What force keeps all the objects in the universe in perpetual motion?

Scientists tell us that the force that could account for all the motion in the universe is the force of the big bang. The big bang is the original event out of which the universe was formed. It happened anywhere from fifteen to twenty billion years ago. The energy from the big bang is the energy that put the universe in motion.

Scientists do not know where the original energy came from. However, they do know that regardless of where it came from, that force is still with us.

It's Raining Cats and Dogs

This saying is often used when rain is coming down in torrents. But what in the world do cats and dogs have to do with rain?

As recently as 1984, during a rainstorm, parts of London were covered with fish that fell from the sky. In 1930, snails, clams, insects, and water plants fell from above during a storm. Other similar events have been documented by scientists the world over.

How does it happen?

Tornadoes have the capability to lift objects. They appear when warm air rises. The rising air causes a low-pressure system on the ground. Air around the low-pressure system gets sucked into the warm rising air. This movement gives the air lift as well as spin. If the suction is strong enough, snails, fish, and crabs—not to mention cats and dogs—may be lifted up into the air.

Fortunately, the average tornado lasts for only minutes in any one place.

However, you probably have heard this other saying, "What goes up must come down." If a plant or animal is lifted into the air by a tornado in one part of the city, it may very well come down in some other part.

Hence, the saying, "It's raining cats and dogs." It has happened.

Nature Abhors a Vacuum

This proverb, attributed to Plutarch, A.D. 46–120, basically means that if a space is empty, nature will try to fill it.

Scientists still believe the proverb to be true; however, they have yet to demonstrate it. Science still has not been able to create a vacuum.

As far as naturally occurring vacuums are concerned (in places such as between the orbitals of electrons and between atoms of hydrogen in deep space), they can only be theorized. This is because, strictly speaking, a vacuum would contain nothing. But then the old philosophical problem pops up: Namely, if a vacuum contains nothing, then nothing exists. But if nothing exists, it is something. If a vacuum contains something, it is not a vacuum, because it contains something called nothing.

Confusing, isn't it?

"Nature abhors a vacuum." Perhaps that's why scientists have been unable to create or even find one.

Twinkle, Twinkle, Little Star
How I Wonder What You Are

The rhyme pinpoints a common problem of sky watchers. At first glance, both stars and planets look alike; they both look like dots of light in the sky.

How can we know the difference?

If it twinkles, it's a star. A star twinkles because it produces its own light. Some of its light gets scattered by our atmosphere. One reason this happens is because the atmosphere is constantly moving. An analogy would be to try to pass a beam of light from a flashlight through a pane of glass held by a friend. As the friend moved the glass, some of the light would be reflected back into your eyes. In other words, by moving the glass, the friend would cause a "twinkle." When stars twinkle, the same thing happens. The beam of light bounces off our atmosphere, as it would off a moving pane of glass.

Planets, on the other hand, do not twinkle.

Planets don't produce their own light. Therefore, planetary light is not in the form of a beam. It is light that is already scattered. Since the light from the planets is scattered to begin with, planets don't twinkle.

Therefore, if a point of light in the sky twinkles, you don't need to wonder what it is.

Under the Weather

When we're "under the weather," we don't feel well.

But does weather actually affect our health?

Researchers have discovered that changes in weather can adversely affect some people. For instance, people with rheumatoid arthritis may feel ill whenever the weather changes from dry to damp. Scientists believe the feeling of illness is due to the change in atmospheric pressure. Affected cells release toxins when the pressure of the atmosphere changes.

Such people are quite literally under the influence of the weather.

Red Sky at Dawn, Sailor Be Warned
Red Sky at Night, Sailor's Delight

This saying appears in the New Testament, Matthew, XVI:2–3: "When it is evening, ye say, it will be fair weather; for the sky is red. And in the morning, it will be foul weather today; for the sky is red and lowering."

Air masses tend to move from the west to the east. The sun sets in the west. Whatever its color, at dusk the air we see is colored by the sun setting in the west.

If the light from the sun passes through dry air, the sky appears to be reddish. Therefore, the next day the dry air will reach us. It will not rain.

On the other hand, if the light from the sun passes through moist air, the sky appears grayish or yellowish. It may rain.

The proverb is true.

OBSERVATIONS

Every Cloud Has a Silver Lining

Optimists love this proverb. Your troubles are only temporary, everything will work out, is the meaning.

The lining of storm clouds may be silver; however, the undersides of the clouds themselves are black. This is because they are full of water. They are so thick and dense that light is unable to penetrate them. For this reason, they look dark and ominous.

The proverbial silver lining, therefore, does not necessarily foretell good weather.

Quite the contrary.

That is, unless you are in the middle of a drought.

A Chain Is No Stronger Than Its Weakest Link

This proverb is attributed to Arthur Conan Doyle's character Sherlock Holmes, who, in 1887, said, "No chain is stronger than its weakest link." He was hunting a gang of criminals. His strategy was to go after the most vulnerable one. This criminal led Holmes to the others. Holmes represented the new, scientific Victorian man. But Holmes's statement actually makes scientific sense.

If two forces are pulling a chain in opposite directions, the chain will not break at any old link. It will break at the link that is slightly thinner than the others, or maybe where it has an invisible crack. In other words, it would be possible to predict exactly where a chain will break.

The proverb implies that we too can predict where it is best to attack certain problems. Solve a problem starting with the most obvious fault, and the rest of the solution may fall into place.

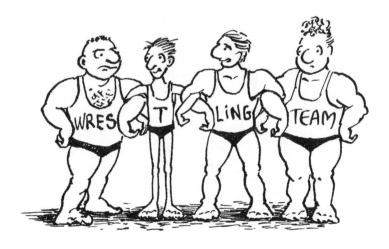

Good Vibrations

"Good, good, good . . . good vibrations."

The song "Good Vibrations" made the Beach Boys famous. Since the Sixties, when the song was a hit, people have used these terms to talk about feelings in general— good vibrations are good feelings and bad vibrations are bad feelings.

Without the vibrations of air molecules, we could not hear music, words, or any other sounds. But good vibrations can become bad vibrations pretty quickly.

For instance, hearing specialists have warned that rock musicians (such as the Beach Boys) as well as airport workers and jack-hammer operators should be particularly careful about certain vibrations.

Loud vibrations could cause loss of hearing. When we hear anything, tufts of hairs that stand up from sensory cells in the inner ear are pushed back and forth. The rocking of the sensory cells produces a neurotransmitter that stimulates the auditory nerve that signals the brain.

Harvard physiologist Charles Liberman thinks that stress due to prolonged exposure to loud sounds damages the roots of these tufts of hairs. Eventually the hairs break at the roots. If this happens, the auditory cell that is attached to these tufts of hairs receives no signal. It cannot respond to *any* vibrations at all. The result of this kind of damage could be permanent loss of hearing.

Good vibrations, in other words, become bad vibrations if they are too loud, and are endured for too long a period of time.

A Rose by Any Other Name Would Smell As Sweet

Changing the name of a person or thing does not alter the nature of that person or thing. That is what Shakespeare was implying when he wrote this phrase in the play *Romeo and Juliet*. The great bard may have had a point about names and people, but his choice of metaphor was a little off base. Roses do not all smell alike.

In fact, one of the most difficult things for rose breeders to do is to incorporate the fragrance of one rose into a different, hybrid rose.

Some of the most fragrant roses, such as Fragrant Cloud, Granada, and Perfume Delight, have not successfully passed on their sweet smells to their hybrid offspring. However, the rose Chrysler Imperial passed its fragrance on to a rose named Jadis, but then Jadis couldn't pass on anything at all. Jadis turned out to be infertile.

Since plenty of genetic material is available to work with, rose breeders are optimistic that someday one rose will smell as sweet as another, no matter what it is called.

For the moment, however, a rose by any other name does not smell as sweet, no matter what Shakespeare said.

Everything Has Its Place

This proverb suggests that there is a reason for everything that exists. But what about viruses? Considering all the diseases they cause, what possible reason could there be for their existence?

According to Drs. Jed Fuhrman and Lita Proctor of the University of Southern California, life would be unbearable, if not impossible, without them. This is because viruses control the bacteria that fill our oceans.

Bacteria reproduce as fast as every twenty minutes. This rate of reproduction means that the number of bacteria doubles every twenty minutes. In only twenty-four hours, a single bacterium could produce millions of offspring.

Fuhrman and Proctor wondered why seawater, which is a breeding place for bacteria, does not contain more bacteria than it does. They discovered that viruses (a single teaspoon of seawater contains as many as 500 million viruses!) kill about seventy percent of the bacteria in the ocean. If these viruses were not present, the ocean would become a rotten, smelly mess in a very short time.

Another mystery Fuhrman and Proctor are working on is what controls virus numbers. One possibility is that since the viruses are killing their bacterial hosts, the death of bacteria naturally limits virus numbers. Another possibility is that there is something out there that is actively destroying viruses.

There may be a place for virus killers, too, say Fuhrman and Proctor.

Art Is Long, Life Is Short

This ancient proverb dates back to the fifth century B.C. in Greece.

On the surface, the point is clear. Many Greek statues are still with us, but the sculptors who made them are long gone.

However, if we look at the proverb scientifically, we get a different view. Art goes back about fifteen thousand years. Early cave paintings and carvings on tools are the first examples of known art.

This period of time may seem long; however, compare it to the history of life.

Life began about three billion years ago. At that time, single-celled organisms made their appearance on this planet.

When compared to art, life is long.

Groundhogs Can Predict the Weather

On Groundhog Day, February 2, the groundhog, or woodchuck, supposedly comes out of its burrow and examines its shadow. If the animal sees its shadow, the sight apparently causes it to go back into its burrow for another six weeks. This event is supposed to indicate that winter will last at least six more weeks.

On the other hand, if the groundhog does not see its shadow, it stays out. This is supposed to indicate that the winter is over or nearly so.

To date, no one has found even the slightest shade of truth in this shadowy saying.

How Sweet It Is!

This saying originated on the "Jackie Gleason" show. However, Gleason had no real inkling about how sweet things could get.

Claude Nofre and Jean-Marie Tinti of the Claude Bernard University in Lyon, France, have created the sweetest substance in the world. The two scientists work for the same company that developed Nutrasweet.

Just how sweet is it?

A single teaspoon of this new substance tastes as sweet as 200,000 teaspoons of sugar!

The substance, which remains unnamed, will be available to the general public when it receives approval from the Federal Drug Administration.

When that happens, we will *all* have a chance to see how sweet it is.

Roses Are Red, Violets Are Blue . . .

Rich Jorgensen, Director of Horticultural Research at DNA Plant Technology in Oakland, California, wondered why violets, petunias, and morning glories come in blue, but roses do not. He speculated that at one time roses might have been blue and that they lost the blue-controlling gene as they evolved. He decided he could put the hypothetical lost gene back.

Jorgensen plans to replace part of the DNA (deoxyribonucleic acid, the stuff of which genes are made) of a rose with some of the DNA of a blue petunia. To do so, he hopes to enlist the help of a bacterium called *Agrobacterium tumefaciens*.

Jorgensen first will splice DNA from a blue petunia into the bacterial DNA. Then he plans to infect a rose with it. If all goes as planned, blue-petunia DNA will replace the red-rose DNA, and the world's first-known blue rose will be his to patent and to sell.

Then the first part of the famous rhyme may be: "Roses are blue, and violets are too."

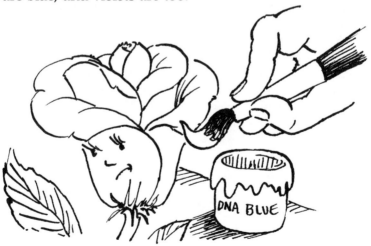

Cats Always Land on Their Feet

This saying refers to the fact that cats possess one of the best gyroscopes in the animal kingdom.

Gyroscopes are used on space vehicles and airplanes to help keep them upright. A cat's gyroscope is built into its ears.

When needed, the information from the "gyroscope" is almost instantly transmitted to the muscles of the cat, which twist it around.

However, the cat needs enough time to turn around.

If there is enough time, cats always land on their feet.

Still Waters Run Deep

This proverb dates back to 1400 in England. Now it is used to assert that a quiet or placid exterior may not reveal all that is going on within a person—strong emotions or passions may be hidden underneath.

Sometimes actual still bodies of water can be deceptive, too.

If a stream of cold water runs into a body of warm water, the cold stream sinks below the warm water. This happens because cold water is slightly more dense than warm water.

A person witnessing such an occurrence would not see anything special going on. On the surface, the body of water would seem very still. However, a fish or an underwater diver might experience a powerful underwater current.

Death Is Sure to All

Some living things are exceptions even to this seemingly ironclad rule. Take, for example, a living amoeba.

Amoebas are single-celled organisms that have existed on earth for more than two billion years. They have a very straightforward way of reproducing. They reproduce by binary fission. In other words, they reproduce by splitting in two.

If you give this method of reproduction a little thought, you realize its odd consequences. The first amoeba appeared on earth some two billion years ago, and it reproduced by splitting in half. Its offspring also reproduced by splitting in half. Hence, an amoeba that is alive today is the result of countless billions of acts of binary fission.

None of its ancestors died. This is true of all creatures that reproduce by binary fission.

Since amoebas reproduce this way, they have no parents (unless you want to say that they are their own parents). In other words, not only do they never die, but they were never born.

One Bad Apple Spoils the Barrel

This proverb serves as a warning to "good people" everywhere. Allow one undesirable person to become part of a nice group of people, and the entire group may stray from its ideals.

But, literally, does one bad apple cause all the other apples in a barrel to become rotten? To answer this question, you have to understand the "behavior" of apples.

Apples tend to be followers.

They "listen" for a message, act on it, and then pass the message on. The message they receive and then produce is in the form of a chemical called ethylene.

Ethylene changes apples in a number of ways. It changes the starches in apples to simpler sugars. This change causes apples to taste sweet. Ethylene also produces an enzyme called cellulase. Cellulase breaks down cellulose. Cellulose gives fruits like apples their crunchiness.

Cellulase, in other words, causes fruit to become soft. The more ethylene produced, the quicker a fruit softens. Eventually it becomes rotten.

But how does one apple affect another?

Ethylene is a chemical signal that is "heard" by other apples. That is to say, if one apple produces ethylene, all the other apples in the barrel detect it and begin to produce ethylene too. Before you know it, all the apples in the barrel are pouring oodles of ethylene into the air—and, so, they all ripen and rot together rather quickly. All of which was caused by a single "bad" apple.

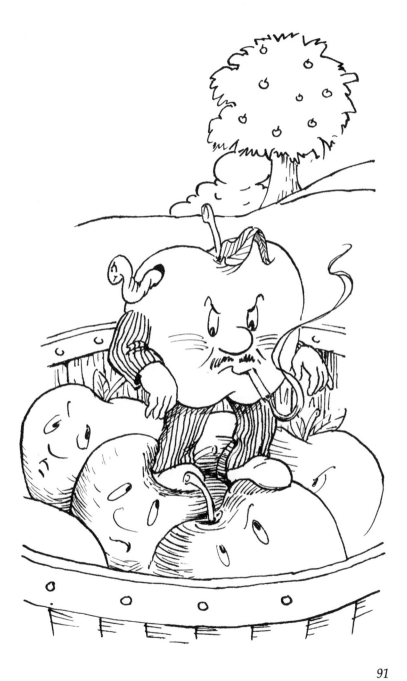

Boys Will Be Boys and Girls Will Be Girls

This proverb dates back to the nineteenth century. It often is used to explain the behavior of boys or of girls as being typical of their gender.

However, in nature, boys sometimes aren't exactly boys. . . .

Take, for instance, the hamlet fish. This fish lives in a coral reef near the West Indies. Whenever it has the urge to mate, this fish has trouble deciding whether boys will be boys, or boys will be girls, or girls will be boys, or. . . .

What happens is that, when one hamlet fish mates with another, the "male" wraps its body around the "female" and helps squeeze out "her" eggs. Then "he" deposits sperm on the eggs. Here we have a clear case of "boys being boys and girls being girls."

Now comes the tricky part.

After about five minutes, the "female," which just laid the eggs, wraps "her" body around what used to be the male. Eggs are squeezed from "him," and "she" deposits sperm on the eggs.

Confusing, isn't it?

The hamlet fish, alas, is a true hermaphrodite; it possesses both male and female organs.

Among the hamlet fish, the proverb should be "Boys will be boys and girls, and girls will be girls and boys."

Ring True

In the Middle Ages, a way to differentiate between a genuine coin and a counterfeit one was to drop it on a stone or tap it with a metal hammer. If the coin did not sound right, did not "ring true," it was judged to be counterfeit. This method depends on properties shared by all metals.

Every metal is composed of atoms arranged in a definite pattern. Change the kind of atoms and, among other things, the pattern changes. For instance, the distance between the atoms may change. The relationship of one atom to another may also change.

Substituting one atom for another causes the sound of the substance it is in to change. Thus, the substitute simply would not ring true.

Today, we use the expression when something seems false about a statement or a story.

The Weeds Overgrow the Corn

This proverb implies that status does not always determine success. Weeds are lower in status than corn; however, they grow faster.

But why should weeds overgrow corn or any other crop for that matter? The reason is simple: Weeds belong where they grow; corn ordinarily does not.

If corn, tomatoes, or most other vegetables were as suitable for the environment as weeds, they would need no extra help from the farmer.

The farmer spends a lot of time and money forcing a crop to grow in a place that is not quite right for it. So, weeds can overgrow corn because they have the blessing of nature.

For nature, weeds are the plants of choice.

The Greatest Events Arise from Accidents

Four great accidents immediately come to mind.

Isaac Newton, the most famous scientist of the seventeenth century, happened to be sitting under an apple tree when he was accidentally struck on the head by an apple. This serendipitous event led to his discovery of the laws of gravity.

The Scottish physician Alexander Fleming discovered penicillin in 1928 by accident. He had been investigating *staphylococci* bacteria (they cause "staph" infections). One of the cultures he was investigating accidentally became contaminated with the fungus *Penicillium*. He noticed that bacterium near the growing fungus was destroyed by it. From this observation, he discovered antibiotics, which turned out to be the most important discovery thus far in the history of medicine.

The French scientist Henri Becquerel also made his great contribution to science by accident. He had left some photographic plates in a drawer, then placed a mineral that contained what he thought was only fluorescent material in the same drawer. Some time later, he found that the so-called fluorescent material had ruined the photographic plates in the drawer—the plates were exposed! Becquerel had discovered radioactivity. Had the photographic plates not been present in the drawer, he might not have discovered radioactivity.

In the 1970s, Dr. Fyodorov of the Soviet Union discovered a cure for nearsightedness by accident. He treated a young man who had gotten slivers of glass in his eye. After the cuts healed, the young patient not only fully recovered from the cuts, but his myopia was also cured.

Dr. Fyodorov studied this accident and perfected it. The procedure he perfected is called radial keratotomy.

However, if you think about it, the proverb is undoubtedly as false as it is true. We will never know how many great discoveries were *not* made because of accidents!

Like Father, Like Son

There are many cases in which a son turns out to be just like his father, not only in his looks, but also in his behavior. However, when it comes to cats, the saying "Like father, like son" has a special significance.

Zoologists at Cambridge University in England wanted to see if friendliness is inherited from the mother or the father cat. They found that it made no difference whether or not a kitten's mother was friendly. Friendliness in both male and female offspring was *never* inherited from her.

According to the zoologists, whether or not a cat is friendly depends entirely on the father. Friendly kittens had friendly fathers; unfriendly kittens did not.

In other words, "Like father, like son" is quite literally true, if you are a cat. Only it should be: "Like father, like son *or daughter.*"

Stick and Stones Will Break My Bones But Names Will Never Hurt Me

This children's proverb is meant to protect a child from unnecesary conflict. It tells a child to ignore the rude words of others, because rude words are not nearly as harmful as being struck by someone.

This advice is good for the child. However, it is not always so in the animal kingdom. For instance, sometimes fish had better heed the "rude words" of dolphins.

Dolphins communicate by sending each other a series of clicks or whistles. Some dolphin sounds are parts of songs, others are danger signals, and still others are just ways of saying hello. Dolphins also hunt with sounds. They sometimes use sounds as powerful weapons.

These sound-weapons are ultrasonic. If you were underwater when the sound was produced, you would not hear it. However, this would not be true if you were a fish. Fish hear dolphin sounds loud and clear.

As a matter of fact, the ultrasonic scream of a dolphin is so loud that it often confuses the fish at which it is aimed. Before the fish has had a chance to figure out what has happened, the dolphin has it for dinner.

Cats Hide Their Claws

This proverb is a warning: A person may seem harmless enough, but he or she may be deceiving you. The person may be hiding wicked intentions.

However, in the case of a cat's retractable claws, deception is not the thing. When its prey sees the cat coming, it "knows" about its claws even if it cannot see them.

Then why do cats "hide their claws"?

Retractable claws are an adaptation. Cats need long claws to grasp or hook prey on the run. On the other hand, cats need to run very fast to catch their prey. If a cat could not retract its claws, its nails would break in the chase. Hence, the need for retractable claws.

Cats do not hide their claws; they save them.

The Milkweed Closes at Night If It Is Going to Rain

This saying turns out to be true.

The same saying can be applied to the clover, dandelion, and pimpernel. These plants have the ability to change leaf angle on the approach of rain.

There is an English version of this saying:

> *Pimpernel, pimpernel, tell me true*
> *Whether the weather be fine or no.*

Perhaps this is why the pimpernel is sometimes referred to as the "poor man's weather glass."

Other plants can also be used as weather instruments. The laurel and the rhododendron can be used as thermometers. Both change leaf angle according to temperature.

The Straw that Broke the Camel's Back

"The straw that broke the camel's back" is the "last straw." It refers to the last thing that happens before a person finally says, "All right, I've had enough. Now I've got to do something." This saying comes from seventeenth-century England.

But would it actually be possible to break the back of a camel with a single piece of straw?

With the help of a computer, scientists probably could figure out exactly how much weight a particular camel could carry. For instance, they could find out how much the animal weighs, how muscular it is, and so on.

They could then figure out the absolute maximum amount that the standing animal could carry on a given day. A single extra gram would literally be the straw that would cause the animal to collapse.

However, no single straw could crack a camel's back. Backbones, or vertebrae, are among the most sturdy in a mammalian body. A camel standing up would simply bend its knees before its vertebrae even felt the stress.

This, of course, is theoretical, since camels are loaded when they are in the sitting position.

What Goes Up Must Come Down

You will see by the following examples that this proverb does not hold up.

Under water, not everything that goes up must come down. For instance, a diver's bubbles climb up to the water's surface but do not come down. Anything less dense than water will do the same.

The proverb is also gravity-dependent. Since gravity does not exist (for all intents and purposes) in space, the proverb would not be true there either. For this reason, astronauts must have special toilets and showers. They even need special foods that don't produce crumbs, which would quickly go up into the cabin of their space vehicle never to come down.

Even on the earth's surface, some things that go up do not come down. For instance, the helium we use to fill up children's balloons is lighter than air. Therefore, whenever we release helium into the air, it goes straight up, never, ever to come down.

BEHAVIOR

A Cow with Its Tail to the West Makes Weather the Best; A Cow with Its Tail to the East Makes Weather the Least

Have you ever noticed that a herd of cattle often faces in the same direction in a field? Have you ever wondered why?

Cows tend to face the opposite direction to which a wind is blowing. They do this as a form of self-defense. If a predator, such as a wolf, tries to sneak up behind them, they do not need to see it. Since they are downwind with respect to the wolf, they will smell the wolf coming. On the other hand, a wolf can't approach the head end of the cow without risking being seen.

In the eastern part of the United States, where this saying originates, west winds often mean fair weather and east winds often mean rain. So, watching the direction in which a cow is standing also could be used as a means of forecasting the weather.

Man's Best Friend (1)

Dogs are loyal, trustworthy, and affectionate to a fault. And best of all, they don't seem to mind playing second fiddle. With a dog, there is never a question about who is boss. We are the boss as far as they are concerned, and they have no problem with that relationship.

Researchers studying dog behavior have found that there is a reason that dogs behave this way.

People feed, house, and sometimes even protect them. We, in other words, provide for all the dog's needs. In a dog's universe, only one kind of individual is so powerful. That individual is the leader of their pack.

Dogs, in other words, think that people are dogs. Their master is the leader of the pack to which they belong.

Man is dog's best friend.

Man's Best Friend (2)

Dogs take their undisputed place as man's best friend.

But what about cats? Surely there are as many cat lovers as dog lovers. Why aren't cats referred to as "man's best friend"?

Perhaps it has to do with how cats perceive us.

We are our dogs' masters. If we are our cats' masters, no one seems to have informed them about it.

Researchers have studied cat behaviors to find out why cats behave so differently from dogs. They discovered that cats that are raised as kittens by humans reach a rather odd conclusion about themselves. Such cats perceive themselves as human.

Since they are human, subservience is out of the question.

Cats treat people as equals.

A Feather in Your Cap

To have "a feather in your cap" these days is to have something good that you could put in your résumé.

This saying, which dates back to the sixteenth century, refers to the practice of awarding feathers to soldiers in order to honor them. A feather in their cap became part of their uniform. Medals of honor serve the same purpose in today's military.

Some of our fine-feathered friends have such "medals of honor," and they are accorded the appropriate respect by other birds.

Peacocks, for example, are revered for their great array of feathers not only by NBC but by birds as well. But producing such large and beautiful feathers takes a great deal of time and energy.

Why do they do it? Not to end up in some soldier's cap, that's for sure.

Researchers have found that hens prefer males with big, colorful feathers to males with smaller, duller feathers. They mate with the bird with the most beautiful feathers.

Why the great attraction to big feathers? Only a male that is capable of obtaining a lot of food could grow big feathers. Such a male must, in other words, possess powerful traits that enable him to produce great feathers. The hen mates with such a male "hoping" that her chicks will inherit his good traits. Such a match would be a real "feather in her cap."

Cold-Blooded

A murderer is sometimes called a "cold-blooded killer."

The saying means that no feelings were involved in the evil deed. The killer had killed as easily as a cold-blooded snake swallows a mouse.

But do cold-blooded animals have less remorse about killing than warm-blooded ones?

If you have ever seen a lion catch an antelope, an African wild dog take a wildebeest, or a house cat kill a sparrow, I think you know the answer.

Warm-blooded predators are as "cold-blooded" as snakes and lizards when it comes to killing prey for their survival.

Makes My Skin Crawl

If someone or something "makes your skin crawl," evidently a particular person or thing is displeasing you greatly—and you actually "feel" the displeasure in your skin.

Physiologists have a clear explanation for this phenomenon.

It has to do with the hair on your body. Every hair is attached to a tiny muscle. If or when we are subjected to a strong emotion, these muscles may contract. This can cause hairs to stand on end.

The feeling of these hair muscles contracting is probably at the root of "making your skin crawl."

Some situations literally make it happen.

Losing One's Head (1)

"Losing one's head" in an argument means losing control of oneself. What about actually losing one's head? Could one live without it?

At least two scientists investigated this gruesome possibility.

Dr. Ivan Huber of Fairleigh Dickinson University discovered that decapitated cockroach heads stay alive and continue to respond for up to twelve hours!

In the eighteenth century, Francesco Redi surgically removed the brain from a tortoise. The animal continued to grope its way around for nearly six months before it died. Amazed, Redi performed an autopsy only to find that the skull of the animal was still completely empty.

Astonished by what he discovered and insensitive to the appalling cruelty of his act, Redi tried another experiment. He completely decapitated another tortoise. The animal lived for twenty-three days without its head, before finally expiring.

Losing One's Head (2)

People who "lose their head" *over another person* are either people who have lost their temper or people who are in love. In either case, they are no longer in control of their thoughts or emotions; hence, they have "lost their heads."

The saying is more than mere metaphor for the praying mantis. A male mantis who "loses his head" over a particular female is in for a big surprise.

When the male starts to mate with a female, she grasps the male's head with her forelegs, and then while they are still mating, she bites it off and eats it. Why does she treat her lover so cruelly? For one thing, the head is nutritious.

But why doesn't she wait until he is at least finished mating before killing him? The answer is simple. She "knows" that destruction of the male's brain removes his inhibitory control over copulation. Males who have lost their heads copulate for a much longer time than they do with their heads still in place!

Monkey See, Monkey Do

Although "Monkey see, monkey do" has the negative implication that a person does not think for him- or herself, when the saying is applied to monkeys it becomes a remarkable observation. Monkeys can be trained to do what they see, if the training starts when they are very young.

For instance, the pigtail macaque, *Macaca nemestrina*, of Malaysia is trained from an early age to work for pay.

These animals climb palm trees and search for ripe coconuts. After finding them, they toss them down to older monkeys, which sort them according to size. For their work, the monkeys are paid with bananas.

There is a recorded case in which these monkeys were mistakenly given fewer bananas for their pay. The monkeys actually went to the boss's office and screamed their complaints. They refused to go back to work until the number of bananas agreed upon was given to them.

Capuchin monkeys, *Cebidae*, are trained to help severely handicapped people. Their responsibilities include opening and closing doors, spoon-feeding, turning the pages of a book, and turning on and off the lights in a room.

"Monkey see, monkey do" is a reprimand often given to a child who sees another child do something wrong and then tries it him- or herself. Monkeys could also possibly see a person (or another monkey) do something wrong and then try it themselves. However, there is no recorded case of such behavior.

Sweat It Out

Metaphorically, this expression means to endure a difficult time. Literally, it means to perspire through a period in which you are ill.

Illness sometimes causes sweating. Sweating out a cold is a common remedy. But does it really work?

Sweat is a response to high temperature, including fever. Fever can be a good thing. Fever makes it difficult for bacteria to absorb iron, and bacteria need iron to survive. Fever also increases the number of T cells produced by the body. T cells are in charge of the body's defenses. They help destroy viruses.

Colds and flus are caused by viruses. Therefore, having a fever helps destroy them. So, sweating out a cold or flu could be a good thing.

Why, then, do doctors prescribe medicines to lower fever? Fever not only destroys germs, but it also interferes with normal body functions. High temperatures, for instance, interfere with cell metabolism. High enough temperatures could cause brain damage or even death.

Physicians, therefore, have to balance the benefits of having a fever against the possible disadvantages that come with it. Sometimes a fever is more of a problem than the microbe causing it. In this case, the adverse side effects of fever rule out any thought of sweating out the illness.

Being a Bully

Webster's Dictionary defines "bully" as "a person who hurts, frightens, or tyrannizes over those who are smaller or weaker."

But are bulls actually "bullies"?

Ask any dairy or beef rancher and you will be told that most bulls are not very nice. For example, a typical bull butts and assaults a heifer into mating. Bulls simply are bigger and stronger than heifers and take advantage of the fact. Hence, bulls well deserve their reputations.

Most bulls are "bullies."

Stool Pigeon

"Stool pigeons" are traitors. They betray the group they belong to. But why associate pigeons with traitors? Why not sparrows or hummingbirds?

In the nineteenth century, pigeon was an English delicacy. Hunting for pigeon was one way of obtaining the bird. However, the bird was mangled by the shot that killed it. And, among other things, a cook had to be sure to remove all the shot or risk cracking someone's tooth.

Trapping pigeons was a far more sensible alternative to shooting them.

In order to trap them, trappers took advantage of a pigeon adaptation. Like many birds, pigeons tend to flock together. Since they tend to flock, they can be trapped easily.

Trappers would tie a pigeon to the stool that they would bring along to sit upon. When a wild pigeon saw the tied-up pigeon, it would fly down near it and, more often than not, get trapped by the trapper.

The wild pigeon was literally betrayed by the stool pigeon.

Scared Stiff

Becoming so frightened that one cannot move is not uncommon in nature.

Three hundred twenty-five years ago, an Austrian monk demonstrated that if he held a chicken's head to the ground, the chicken would quickly stop struggling and become "stiff as a statue." The chicken would remain in this state for some time, even after the monk let go of its head. Later, people who duplicated the monk's experiment assumed that the chicken was hypnotized. However, it was not hypnotized; it was scared stiff.

This behavior has also been demonstrated in insects, crabs, fish, frogs, snakes, primates, and other animals.

Why do animals become stiff under certain kinds of stress? Charles Darwin thought that animals increased their chances of survival by feigning death. His theory was based upon the observation that many predators will not eat dead prey.

Being scared stiff is a reality in nature; it is evidently an evolved strategy for survival.

The Birds and the Bees

When a person explains about "the birds and the bees," sex is the topic. But why birds and bees?

Bees are a particularly weak choice when it comes to sex. More than ninety-nine percent of all female bees never have sex at all. Only the queen is allowed to reproduce, and she only mates once. When she mates, she stores enough sperm to last her a lifetime.

Birds are great homemakers. But their sex lives are pretty dull. They don't even have reproductive organs most of the time. They shrink when it's not mating season. And their mating season doesn't last that long. They get rid of their reproductive organs to reduce their weight for flight.

So, you can talk about the birds and the bees all you want. However, there wouldn't be all that much to talk about when the subject of their sex lives comes up.

Chew the Fat

What does chewing have to do with fat?

The expression "chew the fat" comes from the time when sailors were fed salt pork on long voyages. They sometimes would be fed very fatty pieces of pork that would have to be chewed a long time to be digested. The reason fat requires so much chewing is that it is made of long chains of molecules that must be broken down before the useful energy for which the fat is eaten can be obtained.

The long time spent at the dinner table chewing fatty pieces of salted pork led to a lot of idle conversation, which is what is implied by the saying.

Seeing Red

When we "see red," we are very angry.

The saying originates from bullfighting. Wave a red cape in front of a bull and he attacks. The bull is "seeing red."

However, researchers have discovered that bulls are actually indifferent to the color red. They are color-blind. Wave a white handkerchief in front of a bull and chances are he will react the same way.

It's not the color red to which he is reacting. It's the audacity of the person waving the cape in his face that causes him to lose his short temper.

Putting One's Best Foot Forward

The question is, however, which foot is one's best foot?

Most of us do not realize it, but right- or left-footedness, like right- and left-handedness, is something about which we have very little choice. Unless we make a conscious effort about putting a certain foot forward, we always take the first step with the same foot.

Most of our four-legged friends are also either right- or left-pawed. If you have a dog, careful observation would show that it always puts the same paw forward when it takes a first step.

Right- or left-footedness is controlled in the same way that right- or left-handedness is controlled. It is genetically programmed from the moment we are conceived. We take after an ancestor who was similarly right- or left-footed.

Putting one's best foot forward metaphorically means giving a particular endeavor our absolute best effort. But depending on the trait we inherited, our best foot could either be the right or left foot.

True Blue

If you are "true blue," it is implied that you are loyal.

In the animal kingdom, many birds are reputed to be "true blue" to their mates. However, recent findings have demonstrated that birds are sometimes as deceptive to their mates as are humans.

For instance, pied flycatchers are nominally monogamous, home-loving birds. However, sometimes appearances can be deceptive.

Some males set up second secret households a couple of hundred yards from their first. As if this weren't enough, they also fly around trying to inseminate the mates of other males that are temporarily absent.

The big loser in this last scenario is not the oft-deceived female but the male. He may squander the whole breeding season feeding chicks that are not his own. However, from the female's point of view, it makes little difference who feeds her precious chicks. She'll not bite the hand that feeds them.

Two's Company, Three's a Crowd

This proverb comes from early-eighteenth-century Spain.

Two people can more easily reach a consensus than three or more is the gist of the saying. It also has implications for lovers, who often wish to be alone.

Canaries take the proverb very seriously.

If you were to put two females in the same cage with a single male, the arrangement seems to make all the birds unhappy. For instance, there is far less singing than when only a mated pair is present. However, if two males are placed in the same cage with a single female, the amount of time spent singing often increases dramatically. This is because the competing males become engaged in a singing contest.

What might they be singing?

"This chick is with me—and two's company, three's a crowd," most likely.

Index